RENO-BENTEEN
ENTRENCHMENT TRAIL

Around the Reno-Benteen Defense Site, second half of the Battle of the Little Bighorn, June 25-26, 1876.

CUSTER BATTLEFIELD
National Monument • Montana

FOR YOUR SAFETY

Beware! This is Rattlesnake country. Please stay on pathways. Because of fire danger in the summer extinguish all smoking material before entering trail.

HELP US PROTECT THE RESOURCES

— Stay on paved trail
— Do not disturb wildlife or vegetation
— Do not deface headstones

Original Text by Dr. Don Rickey
Text Revision by Neil C. Mangum and Dan Martinez. Published by Custer Battlefield Historical & Museum Association, 1981, 1983.
Photographs: Dan Martinez
Illustrations on pages 9, 12, 14 & 15 are courtesy of The Old Army Press.

Custer Battlefield National Monument
P. O. Box 39
Crow Agency, Montana 59022

The Reno-Benteen Entrenchment Trail Custer Battlefield National Monument

The numbered sections in this booklet refer to the numbered posts located along the trail around the defense perimeter. The white stakes along the trail mark locations where groups of empty carbine cartridges were found, indicating positions from which the soldiers were firing. *(See Map on rear of Booklet, P. 20.)*

It was approximately 4 P.M. on a sweltering Sunday afternoon — June 25, 1876, when the remnants of Major Marcus A. Reno's 3 companies reached the bluffs following a disastrous attack in the valley. He was joined by Captain Frederick W. Benteen's 3 companies (125 men) and the pack train (130 men). Reno reorganized and then went in search of Custer whose firing could be discerned to the north in the direction of the present day visitor center.

Getting as far as Weir Point, one mile to the north, Reno was compelled to return to this site where he established his defense line about 7 P.M. Sioux and Cheyenne warriors, now finished with Custer, surrounded the remaining seven companies of the 7th Cavalry and began firing a hail of bullets into the soldiers defense area.

————————◆————————

". . .everybody now lay down and spread himself out as thin as possible. After lying there a few minutes I was horrified to find myself wondering if a small sagebrush, about as thick as my finger, would turn a bullet, so I got up and walked along the line, cautioned the men not to waste ammunition; ordered certain men who were good shots to do the firing, and others to keep them supplied with loaded guns."

Lt. Edward S. Godfrey

THIS AREA WAS
OCCUPIED BY TR—
OOPS A, B, D, G, H,
K, AND M, 7TH. U. S.
CAVALRY, AND THE
PACK TRAIN WHEN
THEY WERE BESIE-
GED BY THE SIOUX
INDIANS JUNE 25TH.
AND 26TH. 1876.

Reno's Skirmish Line   INDIAN   ENCAMPMENT

RENO'S RETREAT

Little Big Horn River

Warriors
Soldiers

Looking down the ravines toward the Little Big Horn River, you see where Maj. Marcus A. Reno led his three companies back across the river in retreat from where he earlier attacked the southern end of the Indian encampment. Hundreds of warriors counterattacked and outflanked Reno's men, forcing them first into the timber and then into retreat here to the bluffs. The defense line at this position was occupied by Capt. Thomas H. French's M Company. McDougall's B Company defended this area on June 26, when French was summoned to support Benteen.

———————— ◆ ————————

"We were not very well entrenched, as I recall that I used my butcher knife to cut the earth loose and throw a mound of it in front of me upon which to rest my carbine . . . a bullet struck the corner of this mound, throwing so much dirt into my eyes that I could scarcely see for an hour or more . . . while lying face down on the ground, a bullet tore off the heel of my left boot as effectively as though it had been sawed off!"

Pvt. William C. Slaper, M Company

Not all the M Company men were so lucky:

"A soldier named (Pat) Golden was . . . beside me. We had been talking at intervals during the battle that afternoon, and when the fighting stopped shortly after dark I started to talk to him again. He didn't answer as I rattled on, and at last when I reached out my hand and touched his head it was covered with blood."

Pvt. Edward Pigford, M Company

Warriors took up positions close to this side of the defense area during the night of June 25 and the early morning of June 26. Capt. Frederick W. Benteen asked for more men, so Captain French brought M Company over to hold this segment of the line on June 26. Indian riflemen were posted behind all the hills and ridges to the west of this position.

The one surviving doctor, Assistant Surgeon Henry R. Porter, collected the wounded and set up an improvised field hospital at the site now marked in the depression between here and the memorial monument. Many of Reno's men had been wounded in the valley fight and retreat, and Indian bullets were taking their toll as other men were hit at several places along the defense lines.

---◆---

". . .Corporal (George) Lell . . . was fatally wounded (in the abdomen) and dragged to the hospital. He was dying, and knew it. "Lift me up boys," he said to some of the men, "I want to see the boys again before I go." So they held him up in a sitting position where he could see his comrades in action . . . then they laid him down and he died soon after . . . I will never forget Corporal Lell."

Pvt. Charles Windolph, H Company

---◆---

This shallow trench was dug under fire the morning of June 26, by some of Captain Benteen's H Company men. Only three or four shovels were available, and much of the digging was done with knives, hatchets, and mess gear. Dead horses and mules were dragged up and laid on the parapet as added cover. These trenches were restored to their original dimensions in an archeological project in June 1958. H Company, with men from other companies, held this most exposed hilltop on the southern part of the defense perimeter.

Using the carbines and ammunition taken from the Custer dead, Indians turned them on Reno and Benteen's force. Indian riflemen occupied all the ridges to the east and southeast of here.

By the morning of June 26, the command had been without water for about 24 hours. The wounded were suffering terribly for lack of water. Doctor Porter advised Major Reno and Captain Benteen that some of the wounded would soon die unless they were given water.

———————— ◆ ————————

"The excitement and heat made our thirst almost maddening. The men were forbidden to use tobacco. They put pebbles in their mouths to excite the glands, some ate grass roots, but did not find relief; some tried to eat hard bread, but after chewing it a while would blow it out of their mouths like so much flour."

Lt. Edward S. Godfrey

". . . the sun beat down on us and we became so thirsty that it was almost impossible to swallow."

Pvt. Jacob Adams, H Company

———————— ◆ ————————

Captain Benteen called for volunteers to go down to the river, in the face of Indian gunfire, to fill kettles and canteens. During the morning, several groups of volunteers went down to the deep ravine in front of this point and obtained enough water to ease the wounded. Four men went down to the edge of the river bluff, above the mouth of the ravine, and stood up, firing their carbines, to keep the Indians from shooting too heavily at the water carriers, and to draw the fire of some of the Indians posted in the brush across the river. These four, and 15 of the volunteer water carriers, later received the Congressional Medal of Honor. Only one of the water carriers was badly wounded in the dash to the river. Pvt. Mike Madden's leg was shattered by a bullet, and he had to be carried back up to the defense position by one of the Crow scouts. Madden's leg was amputated, but he survived the injury and lived for many years. For reasons unknown, he was not awarded the Medal of Honor.

Water Carriers Ravine.

Members of the Volunteer Water Parties, and the
Sharpshooters Who Covered Them

Sharpshooters: Sgt. George H. Geiger, Co. H, Blacksmith Henry W. B.
Mechlin, Co. H, Saddler Otto Voit, Co. H, Pvt. Charles Windolph, Co. H.
Water Carriers: Pvts. Neil Bancroft, Co. A, Pvt. Abraham B. Brant, Co.
D, Pvt. Thomas J. Callan, Co. B, Pvt. Theodore W. Goldin, Co. G, Pvt.
David W. Harris, Co. A, Pvt. Wm. M. Harris, Co. D, Sgt. Rufus D.
Hutchinson, Co. B, Sgt. Stanislaus Roy, Co. A, Pvt. James Pym, Co. B,
Pvt. George D. Scott, Co. D, Pvt. Thomas W. Stevenson, Co. D, Pvt.
Peter Thompshon, Co. C, Pvt. Frank Tolan, Co. D, Pvt. Charles H.
Welch, Co. D, Pvt. Frederick Deitline, Co. D.

A few other Medals of Honor were later awarded to men of the Reno-Benteen command for such brave deeds as retrieving a stampeded pack mule, laden with ammunition, from within the Indian lines; for conspicuous gallantry on the firing line; and for recovering the body of Lt. Benjamin Hodgson from within the Indian lines.

 This L-shaped trench was restored in June 1958. Skeletal remains, buttons and scraps of uniform cloth revealed that two or three men were buried in the trench after the fight was over on June 26. Pvts. Julian Jones and Thomas Meador were killed on the firing line about 35 yards further south along the trail. The remains were most likely those of Jones and Meador.

 Charles Windolph, Congressional Medal of Honor winner and last survivor of the Reno-Benteen contingent, pointed out the places where Jones and Meador were killed. Windolph died at the age of 98, on March 11, 1950.

———————— ◆ ————————

"When the firing commenced in the morning (June 26), I said to Jones, "Let's get off our coats." He didn't move. I reached down and turned him over. He was dead, shot through the heart."

Pvt. Charles Windolph, H Company

A party of warriors crawled up the ravines leading from the river to this point during the night of June 25. The morning of June 26 they were close enough to throw rocks at soldiers holding this end of the line. Realizing that the Indians were threatening to break the defense lines, Captain Benteen led a charge and drove the warriors back.

◆

Looking east, up the tree-lined valley of Reno Creek, (Sundance or Ash Creek) toward the saddle-gap on the mountainous horizon, (Wolf Mountains) you see the route followed by the 7th Cavalry the morning of June 25 on their way to attack the Indian encampment.

Crows Nest

WOLF   MOUNTAINS

E
N ⊕ S
W

Marching Routes
Custer ----------
Reno ....
Benteen ● ● ● ● ●

Captain Benteen organized his desperate counterattack from this point the morning of June 26. Leading his yelling soldiers around the point of the hill to the right, he surprised the Indians threatening the southern end of the defense lines. Only one of Benteen's men was killed in this charge. A young Sioux rushed up from the southeast to count coup by striking the dead soldier, but was shot several times as he ran for the shelter of his own lines, falling near the bottom of this slope.

A makeshift barricade of pack saddles, hardtack boxes, sides of bacon, dead mules and horses, and anything that might possibly turn a bullet were erected by A Company across this gently sloping ravine. Soldiers fought from behind the barricade, and the remains of one of them were discovered in June 1958, where the headboard marker is located. Many horses and mules were killed in this end of the saucer-shaped depression.

Skeletal Remains Discovered in 1958

"The surviving (mules and) horses were arranged in a semi-circle with their saddles and bridles on, the wounded being in the valley, between the horses . . ."

Pvt. Francis J. Kennedy, I Company

——————— ◆ ———————

This position was defended by Company G. Rifle pit, restored to original size in an archeological project in June 1958.

Two restored rifle pits. Lack of tools kept the men of K Company from preparing better defenses. The night of June 25, after the firing stopped for a while, the men:

". . . settled down to the work of digging rifle pits. The men worked in pairs, in threes and fours. The ground was hard and dry. There were only three or four spades and shovels in the whole command; axes, hatchets, knives, table forks, tincups, and halves of canteens were brought into use. However, everybody worked hard, and some were still digging when the enemy opened fire at early dawn. . ."

Lt. Edward S. Godfrey, K Company

These shallow depressions here are original rifle pits, unrestored, after many years of weathering.

 Rifle pit, restored in June 1958 was defended by Company K, June 25 and 26.

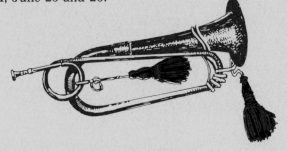

 The granite marker to the left of the trail indicates the site of an 1876 grave pit where the remains of at least one 7th Cavalry man were originally buried. Archeological excavation revealed that most of the remains in the pit were long ago disinterred, probably in 1881 when the mass grave was prepared around the Memorial Shaft on Custer Ridge, 5 miles to the north.

18 Indian sharpshooters occupied vantage points all around the defense area, and especially here, on the northern part of the field. Most warriors were not good marksmen with guns and few owned long-range rifles. However, some Indians did have firearms, and were expert in their use.

"There was a high ridge on the right (600 yards to the northwest) . . . and one Indian in particular I must give credit for being a good shot. While we were lying in the line he fired a shot and killed the fourth man on my right. Soon afterward he fired again and shot the third man. His third shot wounded the man on my right, who jumped back from the line, and down among the rest of the wounded. I thought my turn was coming next. I jumped up, with Captain French, and some half a dozen members of my company, and, instead of firing straight to the front, as we had been doing . . . we wheeled to our right and put in a deadly volley, and I think we put an end to that Indian, as there were no more men killed at that particular spot."

1st Sgt. John M Ryan, M Company

RESCUE AND RETREAT . . . A Postscript

The Indian encampment moved off to the south and southwest toward the Bighorn Mountains in the distance. On the evening of June 26, the Reno Benteen battalions were unsure of their sudden departure. Many suspected a trick on the Indians part and the soldiers spent another weary night on the bluffs. Early the next morning, the nearly exhausted soldiers spied a large dust cloud in the river valley to the north, and soon learned that General Terry, with Col. John Gibbon's infantry and cavalry column, was marching up the river. This was the reason the Indians had abandoned the siege.

"I never saw anything in all my life that looked as good to me as Terry's men."

Pvt. Edward Pigford

From A Picture Report of the Custer Fight, Copyright 1967 by William Reusswig, permission by Hastings House, Publishers.

From A Picture Report of the Custer Fight, Copyright 1967 by William Reusswig, permission by Hastings House, Publishers.

The relieving troops camped on the sagebrush flats on the west side of the river. Below these bluffs, General Terry rode into the Reno-Benteen Defense Site, bringing the first news of the death of Lt. Col. George A. Custer and the other five companies of the regiment. The Reno-Benteen command moved down and camped with the relief troops. The Custer dead were counted and covered up, and the remnants of the 7th Cavalry accompanied the Terry-Gibbon column back down the Little Bighorn to its mouth, where the badly wounded were placed on board the steamer *Far West*. The Battle of the Little Bighorn had passed into history.

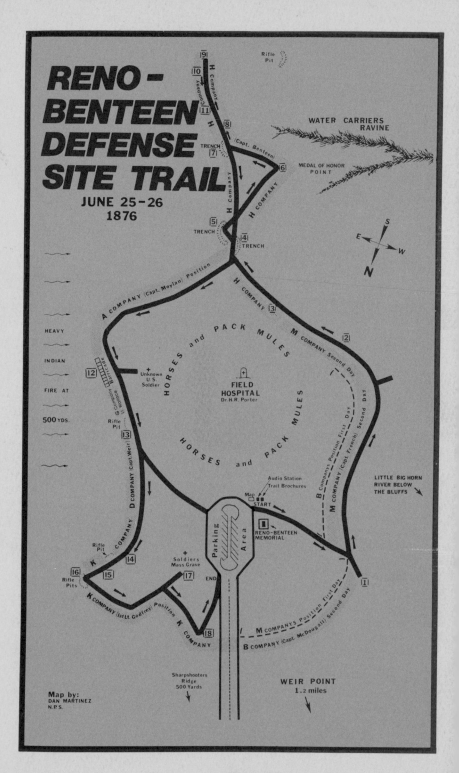